CLIMB the Summer Slide
1st level

Climb the Summer Slide

Read

The day was not gone before he had a great fright. He tumbled out of the apple tree and fell squawking and fluttering upon the ground.

Copy the sentence. (The day was not gone before he had a great fright.)

_____

_____

_____

Language Arts

What's wrong with the sentence?

I like green eggs and ham

Math

$4 + 5 =$ 　　　　　　　$3 + 5 =$

$5 - 2 =$ 　　　　　　　$9 - 6 =$

What's next in the pattern? Draw the shape.

     _____

Read

Upon his arrival, as a stranger, in Pleasant Valley, Solomon Owl looked about carefully for a place to live. What he wanted especially was a good, dark hole, for he thought that sunshine was very dismal.

Copy the sentence. (Owl looked about carefully for a place to live.)

_____

_____

_____

Language Arts

Underline the proper noun. What pronoun would you replace it with?

Sarah likes eggs and ham. _____

Math

3 + 4 =   4 + 2 =

5 − 0 =   7 − 5 =

What time is it?

_____ o'clock

Let's countdown 40, 39...

Read

Isn't it funny how two people will often think of the same thing at the same time, and neither one know that the other is thinking of it? That is just what happened the day that Buster Bear first thought of going berrying. While he was walking around in the Green Forest, talking to himself about how hungry he was for some berries and how sure he was that there must be some up in the Old Pasture, someone else was thinking about berries and about the Old Pasture too.

Copy the sentence. (Isn't it funny?)

_____

_____

Language Arts

Circle the proper nouns.

beach   California   happiness   Elle

Math

$3 + 3 =$ $4 + 3 =$

$5 - 4 =$ $6 - 4 =$

Draw a picture that shows the fraction three fourths.

$$\frac{3}{4}$$

Let's countdown 40, 39, 38...

Read

Mrs. Woodpecker flew to her neighbor Mrs. Flicker's tree and rapped, tap-tap-tap-tap. She didn't rap gently, either. She was not in a gentle mood. She intended to find out why Mrs. Flicker had called to Reddy Woodpecker, "Good morning, my dear!" Mrs. Flicker promptly stuck her head out of her door.

Copy the sentence. (Mrs. Flicker promptly stuck her head out of her door.)

_____

_____

_____

Language Arts

Which is the correct spelling of the plural?

box   boxs   boxes   boxen

Math

$1 + 5 =$ $3 + 5 =$

$7 - 4 =$ $6 - 3 =$

How many dimes do you need to make forty cents?

Let's countdown 40, 39, 38, 37...

Climb the Summer Slide

Read

Peter was most dreadfully frightened; he rushed all over the garden, for he had forgotten the way back to the gate. He lost one of his shoes among the cabbages, and the other shoe amongst the potatoes.

Copy the sentence. (Peter was most dreadfully frightened.)

_____

_____

Language Arts

What's wrong with the sentence?

i do like green eggs and ham.

Math

$4 + 5 =$ $\qquad\qquad$ $2 + 5 =$

$7 - 3 =$ $\qquad\qquad$ $10 - 5 =$

What's next in the pattern? Draw the shape.

     _____

Read

Life is always a game of hide and seek to Danny Meadow Mouse. You see, he is such a fat little fellow that there are a great many other furry-coated people, and almost as many who wear feathers, who would gobble Danny up for breakfast or for dinner if they could.

Copy the sentence. (Life is always a game of hide and seek to Danny.)

_____

_____

_____

Language Arts

Circle the letters that should be capitalized.

do you shop at walmart?

Math

$$3 + 5 =$$ $$4 + 2 =$$

$$9 - 4 =$$ $$8 - 5 =$$

What time is it?

_____

Let's countdown 40, 39, 38, 37, 36, 35...

Read

For some time Solomon Owl had known that a queer feeling was coming over him. And he could not think what it meant. He noticed, too, that his appetite was leaving him. Nothing seemed to taste good any more.

Copy the sentence. (He could not think what it meant.)

_____

_____

Language Arts

Which contraction is correct? Circle it.

cannot   cant'   ca'nt   can't   c'ant

Math

4 + 3 =　　　　　　5 + 5 =

5 − 4 =　　　　　　6 − 2 =

Color the pieces to show the fraction one half.

 $\frac{1}{2}$

Read

"You're mistaken," Mr. Frog told him. "I haven't written a word. I asked you to come here because you look like a customer. It's good business to have customers seen about my shop. I haven't had a real customer this season," he added somewhat sadly. "So you can't blame me if I want people to think I have one at last now can you?"

Copy the sentence. (I asked you to come here because it's good business.)

_____

_____

_____

Language Arts

Which is the correct spelling of the plural?

wish   wishs   wishes   wishen

Math

$2 + 4 =$ $4 + 4 =$

$8 - 3 =$ $9 - 5 =$

How many nickels do you need to make twenty cents?

Let's countdown 40, 39, 38, 37, 36, 35, 34, 33...

Read

Usually he did his work quickly. But now after every five stitches that he put into his work he stopped to take out ten. And naturally he was not getting on very fast. He had been working busily since early morning; and Jasper Jay's suit was further than ever from being finished.

Copy the sentence. (Usually he did his work quickly.)

_____

_____

Language Arts

What's wrong with the sentence?

Why do you like green eggs and ham.

Math

$5 + 4 =$ $4 + 3 =$

$7 - 4 =$ $8 - 5 =$

What's next in the pattern? Draw the shape.

     _____

Let's countdown 40, 39, 38, 37, 36, 35, 34, 33, 32...

Climb the Summer Slide

Read

Peter was thinking of that young orchard now, as he sat in the moonlight trying to make up his mind where to go. The thought of those young peach trees made his mouth water.

Copy the sentence. (Peter was thinking of that young orchard.)

_____

_____

Language Arts

Circle the three letters that should be capitalized.

turn right at fox road.

Math

$5 + 3 =$ 　　　　　　　　$2 + 2 =$

$7 - 3 =$ 　　　　　　　　$8 - 3 =$

What time is it?

_____

Let's countdown 40, 39, 38, 37, 36, 35, 34, 33, 32, 31...

Climb the Summer Slide

Read

We found such beautiful ones. Some wore purple, some pink, and some brown. When they were spread out in the water, the purple ones looked like plumes, and the brown ones like little trees.

Copy the sentence. (We found such beautiful ones.)

_____

_____

Language Arts

What does the contraction mean?

He's   he will   he is   he would

Math

5 + 2 =   3 + 4 =

6 – 4 =   7 – 2 =

Color the pieces to show the fraction one quarter.

 $\frac{1}{4}$

Read

Peter was worried, so worried that he couldn't go to sleep as he usually does in the daytime. So he sat hidden in the old wall and waited and watched. By and by he saw Farmer Brown and Farmer Brown's boy come out into the orchard. Right away they saw the mischief which Peter had done, and he could tell by the sound of their voices that they were very, very angry.

Copy the sentence. (Peter was so worried that he couldn't sleep.)

_____

_____

Language Arts

Which is the correct spelling of the plural?

fly   flys   flyes   flies

Math

7 + 5 =   3 + 8 =

9 − 2 =   15 − 6 =

How many pennies do you need to make five cents?

Read

When the blazing sun is set,
And the grass with dew is wet,
Then you show your little light;
Twinkle, twinkle, all the night.

Copy the sentence. (When the blazing sun is set, then you show your light.)

_____

_____

_____

Language Arts

What's wrong with the sentence?

I do so like green egges and ham.

Math

6 + 4 =   8 + 5 =

10 − 7 =   8 − 4 =

What's next in the pattern? Write the number.

5, 10, 15, 20, 25, 30, 35, 40, 45, 50, _____

Climb the Summer Slide

Read

In a little while Mr. Flicker returned from his trip to the pasture to see the Woodchuck brothers. Hurrying into the orchard he called to Reddy Woodpecker, "They're thinking it over."

Copy the sentence. ("They're thinking it over.")

_____

_____

Language Arts

Circle the letters that should be capitalized.

Our family visited the washington zoo.

Math

$9 + 3 =$ $4 + 7 =$

$12 - 4 =$ $16 - 9 =$

What time is it?

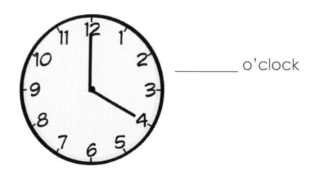

_____ o'clock

Let's countdown 30, 29, 28, 27...

Read

Mr. Crow then muttered something about cousins, and added something more about birds of a feather flocking together. And then he said, "There's the Downy Woodpecker and there's the Hairy Woodpecker both cousins of yours, too. They've only what you might call a touch of red on the backs of their necks; but I suppose..."

Copy the sentence. (Mr. Crow muttered something.)

_____

_____

Language Arts

What does the contraction mean? Circle the answer.

she'll   she will   she could

Math

$8 + 5 =$ $9 + 4 =$

$13 - 4 =$ $11 - 3 =$

Color the pieces to show the fraction one third.

 $\dfrac{1}{3}$

Climb the Summer Slide

Read

Blacky waited until he was sure that no one else was coming. Then he cleared his throat very loudly and began to speak. "Friends," said he.

Everybody grinned, for Blacky has played so many sharp tricks that no one is really his friend unless it is that other mischief-maker, Sammy Jay, who, you know, is Blacky's cousin. But no one said anything, and Blacky went on.

Copy the sentence. (Everybody grinned.)

_____

_____

Language Arts

Which is the correct spelling of the plural?

child   childs   childes   children

Math

60 + 70 =   9 + 5 =

17 − 8 =   10 − 3 =

How many quarters do you need to make fifty cents?

Read

Now, there was a reason for all this chatter. Jolly Robin's wife had seen a handsome stranger in the orchard. And she had hurried away to spread the news among her friends. "He's a dashing person, very elegantly dressed," Mrs. Robin told everybody.

Copy the sentence. (Now, there was a reason for all this chatter.)

_____

_____

_____

Language Arts

What's wrong with the sentence?

I do'nt like green eggs and ham.

Math

$8 + 7 =$ $6 + 9 =$

$16 - 8 =$ $15 - 7 =$

What's next in the pattern? Write the number.

69, 68, 67, 66, 65, 64, 63, 62, 61, 60, _____

Let's countdown 30, 29, 28, 27, 26, 25, 24...

Read

Now having one's own way too much is a bad thing. It is apt to make one selfish and thoughtless of other people and very hard to get along with. Little Joe Otter had his way too much. Grandfather Frog knew it and shook his head very soberly when Little Joe had been disrespectful to him.

Copy the sentence. (Having one's own way too much is a bad thing.)

_____

_____

_____

Language Arts

Circle the letters that should be capitalized.

my family lived in germany for a while.

Math

$4 + 8 =$ $7 + 5 =$

$15 - 8 =$ $13 - 5 =$

What time is it?

_____

Let's countdown 30, 29, 28, 27, 26, 25, 24, 23...

Climb the Summer Slide

Read

Thick and fast things were happening to Danny Meadow Mouse down on the snow-covered Green Meadows. Rather, they were almost happening. He hadn't minded when Reddy Fox all alone tried to catch him. Indeed, he had made a regular game of hide and seek of it and had enjoyed it immensely. But now it was different. Granny Fox wasn't so easily fooled as Reddy Fox. Just Granny alone would have made the game dangerous for Danny Meadow Mouse. But Reddy was with her, and so Danny had two to look out for, and he got so many frights that it seemed to him as if his heart had moved right up into his mouth and was going to stay there.

Copy the name. (Danny Meadow Mouse)

Language Arts

What does the contraction mean? Circle the answer.

we'd   we will   we had

Math

$$60 + 60 =$$ $$7 + 4 =$$

$$18 - 9 =$$ $$12 - 5 =$$

Color the pieces to show the fraction two thirds.

$$\frac{2}{3}$$

Let's countdown 30, 29, 28, 27, 26, 25, 24, 23, 22...

Read

That is what Farmer Brown's boy said when he found that Buster Bear had stolen the berries he had worked so hard to pick and then had run off with the pail. You see, Farmer Brown's boy is learning to be something of a philosopher, one of those people who accept bad things cheerfully and right away see how they are better than they might have been. When he had first heard someone in the bushes where he had hidden his pail of berries, he had been very sure that it was one of the cows or young cattle who live in the Old Pasture during the summer.

Copy the sentence. (That is what Farmer Brown's boy said.)

_____

_____

Language Arts

Which is the correct spelling of the plural?

train   trains   traines   trainen

Math

$8 + 8 =$ $3 + 7 =$

$14 - 7 =$ $12 - 4 =$

How much money do you have? Do you have enough to buy the toy?

    15¢

Let's countdown 30, 29, 28, 27, 26, 25, 24, 23, 22, 21...

Read

Now worry is one of the worst things in the world, and it didn't seem as if there was anything that Danny Meadow Mouse need worry about. But you know it is the easiest thing in the world to find something to worry over and make yourself uncomfortable about. And when you make yourself uncomfortable, you are almost sure to make everyone around you equally uncomfortable.

Copy the sentence. (Now worry is one of the worst things in the world.)

_____

_____

_____

Language Arts

Which words are nouns? Underline them.

I like green eggs and ham.

Math

5 + 8 =   6 + 4 =

15 – 9 =   16 – 7 =

What's next in the pattern? Write the number.

100, 90, 80, 70, 60, 50, 40, 30, 20, _____

Climb the Summer Slide

Read

There are very few of the little people of the Green Forest and the Green Meadows who do not know fear at some time or other, but it comes to Chatterer as seldom as to any one, because he is very sure of himself and his ability to hide or run away from danger.

Copy the sentence. (There are very few people.)

_____

_____

Language Arts

Circle the letters that should be capitalized.

john and joanna are my friends.

Math

$3 + 4 =$ $5 + 2 =$

$9 - 5 =$ $4 - 3 =$

What time is it?

_____

Read

That's a funny thing for hair to do–rise up all of a sudden–isn't it? But that is just what the hair on Farmer Brown's boy's head did the day he went fishing in the Laughing Brook and had no luck at all. There are just two things that make hair rise–anger and fear.

Copy the sentence. (That's just what the hair on Farmer Brown's boy's head did.)

_____

_____

_____

Language Arts

What does the contraction mean? Circle the answer.

I'm   I was   I am   I will

Math

$2 + 3 =$ $5 + 5 =$

$8 - 4 =$ $9 - 4 =$

Color one circle to show one fifths.

$\frac{1}{5}$ ◯ ◯ ◯ ◯ ◯

Let's countdown 20, 19, 18...

Climb the Summer Slide

Read

Now, there was a reason why Jasper spoke in that disagreeable way. He didn't want the story to be true. And, somehow, he felt that if he said it was a hoax, it would really prove to be one.

Copy the sentence. (Now, there was a reason why Jasper spoke that way.)

_____

_____

_____

Language Arts

Which is the correct spelling of the plural?

man   mans   manes   men

Math

$4 + 2 =$ $4 + 4 =$

$8 - 3 =$ $6 - 2 =$

How much money do you have? Do you have enough to buy the toy?

      19¢

Let's countdown 20, 19, 18, 17...

Read

<u>Buster Bear yawned as he lay on his comfortable bed</u> of leaves and watched the first early morning sunbeams creeping through the Green Forest to chase out the Black Shadows. Once more he yawned, and slowly got to his feet and shook himself. Then he walked over to a big pine tree, reached as high up on the trunk of the tree as he could, and scratched the bark with his great claws. After that he yawned until it seemed as if his jaws would crack, and then sat down to think what he wanted for breakfast.

Copy the sentence. (He yawned as he lay on his comfortable bed.)

_____

_____

_____

Language Arts

I replaced Buster Bear from the first sentence in the reading with a pronoun in the sentence to copy. What's the pronoun?

_____

Math

$5 + 5 =$ $3 + 2 =$

$6 - 4 =$ $7 - 3 =$

What's next in the pattern? Write the number.

3, 6, 9, 12, 15, 18, 21, 24, 27, 30, 33 _____

Let's countdown 20, 19, 18, 17, 16...

Climb the Summer Slide

Read

Mr. Crow was more than willing. So they flew to the oak and waited for a time. They saw the cows file into the barn, each finding her own place in one of the two long rows of stanchions that faced each other across the wide aisle running the length of the barn. It was through that aisle that the men walked with great forkfuls of hay in the winter time, which they flung down before the cows, who munched it contentedly.

Copy the sentence. (Mr. Crow was more than willing.)

_____

_____

Language Arts

Circle the letters that should be capitalized.

have you read the book heidi?

Math

$$10 + 0 =$$
$$8 + 5 =$$

$$17 - 9 =$$
$$16 - 8 =$$

What time is it?

_____

Let's countdown 20, 19, 18, 17, 16, 15...

Climb the Summer Slide

Read

Living in the orchard as they did, near the farmhouse, Jolly Robin and his wife knew more about Farmer Green's family than any of the other birds in Pleasant Valley, except maybe Rusty Wren. Being a house wren, Rusty was naturally on the best of terms with all the people in the farmhouse.

Copy the sentence. (Rusty was naturally on the best of terms with them all.)

_____

_____

_____

Language Arts

Circle the proper nouns.

Africa   rocking chair   Sam   box

Math

7 + 5 =   9 + 4 =

15 − 4 =   11 − 4 =

Color the circles to show three fifths.

$\frac{3}{5}$ ◯ ◯

Let's countdown 20, 19, 18, 17, 16, 15, 14...

Climb the Summer Slide

Read

During the day, however, Solomon Owl seldom had anything to say — or if he had, he was quiet about it. One reason for his silence then was that he generally slept when the sun was shining. And when most people were sleeping, Solomon Owl was as wide awake as he could be.

Copy the sentence. (One reason for his silence was that he slept by day.)

_____

_____

_____

Language Arts

What's wrong with the sentence?

Is this right way to do it!

Math

$3 + 7 =$ $\qquad$ $6 + 5 =$

$12 - 3 =$ $\qquad$ $13 - 5 =$

How much money do you have? Do you have enough to buy the toy?

30¢

Let's countdown 20, 19, 18, 17, 16, 15, 14, 13...

Read

<u>But Johnnie Green did not seem frightened at all.</u> He set up a great shouting and began to let fly his snowballs as fast as he could throw them. They did not all find the mark. But the very last one struck the silent stranger squarely upon his left ear. And to Jolly Robin's horror, his head toppled off and fell horridly at his feet.

Copy the sentence. (But he did not seem frightened at all.)

_____

_____

_____

Language Arts

I did it again. I replaced a noun with a pronoun in the sentence to copy.

What's the pronoun? _____

Math

$8 + 6 =$ $7 + 5 =$

$15 - 8 =$ $18 - 9 =$

What's next in the pattern? Write the number.

71, 73, 75, 77, 79, 81, 83, 85, 87, 89, _____

Let's countdown 20, 19, 18, 17, 16, 15, 14, 13, 12...

Climb the Summer Slide

Read

Among all the feathered folk on Farmer Green's place the Robin family was perhaps the sorriest. They had a nest of eggs in the orchard, in a crotch of an old apple tree. And it was on just such trees that Reddy Woodpecker spent a great deal of his time, hunting for grubs. Jolly Robin himself might not have paid much heed to Reddy. But Mrs. Robin was a great worrier. Often she worried over nothing at all.

Copy the sentence. (Often she worried over nothing at all.)

_____

_____

Language Arts

Circle the letters that should be capitalized.

who do you say that i am?

Math

$7 + 6 =$ $\qquad$ $8 + 6 =$

$13 - 8 =$ $\qquad$ $16 - 7 =$

Draw three o'clock.

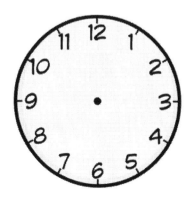

Let's countdown 20, 19, 18, 17, 16, 15, 14, 13, 12, 11...

Climb the Summer Slide

Read

Jemima Puddle-duck was not much in the habit of flying. She ran downhill a few yards flapping her shawl, and then she jumped off into the air. She flew beautifully when she had got a good start.

Copy the sentence. (She ran downhill a few yards flapping her shawl.)

_____

_____

_____

Language Arts

Circle the common nouns.

Europe   books   Disney   friend

Math

6 + 4 =   5 + 7 =

9 − 6 =   12 − 6 =

Color the circles to show two fifths.

$\frac{2}{5}$ ◯ ◯ ◯ ◯ ◯

Read

Solomon's neighbors had been so interested in watching him that they were all sorry when he ceased his strange actions. Indeed, there was a rumor that Solomon had become very angry with Farmer Green and that he was trying to knock down some of Farmer Green's trees. Before the end of that unpleasant week Solomon had often noticed as many as twenty-four of the forest folk following him about, hoping to see a tree fall.

Copy the sentence. (Solomon's neighbors had been so interested.)

_____

_____

Language Arts

What's wrong with the sentence?

I like to have it this way?

Math

$9 + 7 =$ $6 + 9 =$

$16 - 7 =$ $13 - 6 =$

How much money do you have? Do you have enough to buy the toy?

10¢

Climb the Summer Slide

Read

In the middle of the lake there is an island covered with trees and nut bushes; and amongst those trees stands a hollow oak tree, which is the house of an owl who is called Old Brown.

Copy the sentence. (In the middle of the lake there is an island.)

_____

_____

_____

Language Arts

What's the pronoun in this sentence? Underline it.

They like green eggs and ham.

Math

8 + 5 =   7 + 8 =

12 − 5 =   14 − 7 =

What's next in the pattern? Write the number.

98, 96, 94, 92, 90, 88, 86, 84, 82, 80, _____

Let's countdown 10, 9, 8...

Climb the Summer Slide

Read

Over the carpet the dear little feet
Came with a patter to climb on my seat;
Two merry eyes, full of frolic and glee,
Under their lashes looked up unto me;
Two little hands pressing soft on my face,
Drew me down close in a loving embrace;
Two rosy lips gave the answer so true,
"Good to love you, mamma, good to love you."

Copy the line. (Good to love you.)

_____

_____

Language Arts

Circle the letters that should be capitalized.

We go every friday in april.

Math

6 + 7 =   6 + 5 =

13 – 7 =   11 – 3 =

What time is it?

_____ o'clock

Let's countdown 10, 9, 8, 7...

Read

Solomon had so much on his mind that he had no sooner fallen asleep than he awoke again, to study over the question that perplexed him. He certainly did not want Simon to have twice as many mice as he. But Simon's argument was a good one. He had said that since Solomon was more than twice his size, it was proper that he should have a chance to grow.

Copy the sentence. (It was proper that he should have a chance to grow.)

_____

_____

_____

Language Arts

Circle the pronouns.

he   it   friend   all   they   we

Math

$5 + 5 =$ $4 + 8 =$

$15 - 8 =$ $16 - 9 =$

Draw a picture that shows the fraction two thirds.

$$\frac{2}{3}$$

Let's countdown 10, 9, 8, 7, 6...

Read

Some of the birds in Pleasant Valley had long since left for the South. And many of those that hadn't announced that they expected to start for a milder climate that very evening. The weather soon grew warmer. And on the following day Reddy Woodpecker and Frisky Squirrel met at the beech grove.

"These are good nuts, eh?" called Reddy.

Copy the sentence. ("These are good nuts," called Reddy.)

_____

_____

Language Arts

What's wrong with the sentence? There are four mistakes.

weve just started collecting toyes?

Math

$6 + 4 =$ $8 + 9 =$

$12 - 4 =$ $14 - 6 =$

How much money do you have? Do you have enough to buy the toy?

             8¢

Let's countdown 10, 9, 8, 7, 6, 5...

Read

In the middle of the lake there is an island covered with trees and nut bushes; and amongst those trees stands a hollow oak tree, which is the house of an owl who is called Old Brown.

Copy the sentence. (In the middle of the lake there is an island.)

_____

_____

_____

Language Arts

I replaced two nouns in the first sentence with two pronouns in the second. Find them and underline them.

Peter likes ham. He really likes it.

Math

$6 + 7 =$ $8 + 7 =$

$11 - 5 =$ $14 - 6 =$

What's next in the pattern? Write the number.

1, 2, 3, 4, 5, 6, 7, 8, 9, 10, 9, 8, 7, 6, 5,_____

Climb the Summer Slide

Read

A few days later she came home in a dreadful state of mind. "I went to take a look at the raspberry patch," she explained to her good husband. "I knew the berries would soon be ripe. In fact I've had my eye on one that was almost ready to be picked. And what do you think? Right before my own eyes that ruffian Reddy Woodpecker picked it and ate it himself!"

Copy the sentence. (A few days later she came home.)

_____

_____

Language Arts

Circle everything that's wrong with the sentence. Find four things.

i bought those giftes in december?

Math

$$5 + 6 =$$ $$5 + 5 =$$

$$9 - 3 =$$ $$15 - 8 =$$

What time is it?

_____

Let's countdown 10, 9, 8, 7, 6, 5, 4, 3...

Read

"Reddy Woodpecker is taking the food out of our children's mouths!" she wailed. "You'll have to drive him away from the raspberry patch! You'll have to fight him!" Now, Jolly Robin hardly thought that he was a match for Reddy Woodpecker. So when his wife gave him those orders he began to worry, himself.

Copy the sentence. (One reason for his silence was that he slept by day.)

_____

_____

_____

Language Arts

Fill in the pronoun.

_____ is the tallest among her friends.

Math

$9 + 9 =$ $7 + 4 =$

$14 - 5 =$ $8 - 3 =$

Draw a picture that shows three fourths.

$$\frac{3}{4}$$

Let's countdown 10, 9, 8, 7, 6, 5, 4, 3, 2...

Read

Listen to the kitchen clock!
To itself it ever talks,
From its place it never walks;
"Tick-tock-tick-tock: "
Tell me what it says.

Copy the sentence. (Listen to the kitchen clock!)

_____

_____

Language Arts

What's wrong with the sentence?

do you know what youre doing.

Math

8 + 6 =   8 + 9 =

12 − 5 =   17 − 9 =

How much money do you have? Do you have enough to buy the toy?

    60¢

Let's countdown 10, 9, 8, 7, 6, 5, 4, 3, 2, 1!

EP provides free, complete, high quality online homeschool curriculum for children around the world. Find more of our courses and resources on our site, allinonehomeschool.com.

If you prefer offline materials, consider Genesis Curriculum which takes a book of the Bible and turns it into daily lessons in science, social studies, and language arts for your children to learn all together. The curriculum also includes learning Biblical languages. Genesis Curriculum offers Rainbow Readers and A Mind for Math, a math curriculum designed for about first through fourth grade to be done all together. Each math lesson is based on the day's Bible reading from the main curriculum. GC Steps is an offline preschool and kindergarten program. Learn more about our expanding curriculum on our site, GenesisCurriculum.com.

Made in the USA
Middletown, DE
27 March 2023

27791972R00024